12-MONTH · 2024 PLANNER

For I Know the Plans

BELLE CITY GIFTS

Belle City Gifts
Savage, Minnesota, USA

Belle City Gifts is an imprint of BroadStreet Publishing Group LLC.
Broadstreetpublishing.com

For I Know the Plans 2024 Planner

© 2023 by BroadStreet Publishing®

9781424567331

Design and typesetting by Garborg Design Works | garborgdesign.com
Compiled and edited by Michelle Winger | literallyprecise.com

Printed in China.

PERSONAL INFORMATION

Name _____

Address _____

_____

_____

_____

Phone (h) _____

       (w) _____

       (c) _____

Email Address _____

Emergency Contacts _____

_____

_____

Family and Friends _____

_____

_____

_____

_____

_____

_____

_____

_____

_____

2024 AT A GLANCE

JANUARY 2024

S	M	T	W	T	F	S
	1	2	3	4	5	6
7	8	9	10	11	12	13
14	15	16	17	18	19	20
21	22	23	24	25	26	27
28	29	30	31			

FEBRUARY 2024

S	M	T	W	T	F	S
				1	2	3
4	5	6	7	8	9	10
11	12	13	14	15	16	17
18	19	20	21	22	23	24
25	26	27	28	29		

MARCH 2024

S	M	T	W	T	F	S
					1	2
3	4	5	6	7	8	9
10	11	12	13	14	15	16
17	18	19	20	21	22	23
24	25	26	27	28	29	30
31						

APRIL 2024

S	M	T	W	T	F	S
	1	2	3	4	5	6
7	8	9	10	11	12	13
14	15	16	17	18	19	20
21	22	23	24	25	26	27
28	29	30				

MAY 2024

S	M	T	W	T	F	S
			1	2	3	4
5	6	7	8	9	10	11
12	13	14	15	16	17	18
19	20	21	22	23	24	25
26	27	28	29	30	31	

JUNE 2024

S	M	T	W	T	F	S
						1
2	3	4	5	6	7	8
9	10	11	12	13	14	15
16	17	18	19	20	21	22
23	24	25	26	27	28	29
30						

JULY 2024

S	M	T	W	T	F	S
	1	2	3	4	5	6
7	8	9	10	11	12	13
14	15	16	17	18	19	20
21	22	23	24	25	26	27
28	29	30	31			

AUGUST 2024

S	M	T	W	T	F	S
				1	2	3
4	5	6	7	8	9	10
11	12	13	14	15	16	17
18	19	20	21	22	23	24
25	26	27	28	29	30	31

SEPTEMBER 2024

S	M	T	W	T	F	S
1	2	3	4	5	6	7
8	9	10	11	12	13	14
15	16	17	18	19	20	21
22	23	24	25	26	27	28
29	30					

OCTOBER 2024

S	M	T	W	T	F	S
		1	2	3	4	5
6	7	8	9	10	11	12
13	14	15	16	17	18	19
20	21	22	23	24	25	26
27	28	29	30	31		

NOVEMBER 2024

S	M	T	W	T	F	S
					1	2
3	4	5	6	7	8	9
10	11	12	13	14	15	16
17	18	19	20	21	22	23
24	25	26	27	28	29	30

DECEMBER 2024

S	M	T	W	T	F	S
1	2	3	4	5	6	7
8	9	10	11	12	13	14
15	16	17	18	19	20	21
22	23	24	25	26	27	28
29	30	31				

Important Dates

New Year's Day	January 1
Martin Luther King Jr. Day	January 15
Valentine's Day	February 14
Presidents Day	February 19
Daylight Saving Time begins	March 10
St. Patrick's Day	March 17
Spring Equinox	March 19
Palm Sunday	March 24
Good Friday	March 29
Easter Sunday	March 31
National Day of Prayer	May 2
Mother's Day	May 12
Memorial Day	May 27
Father's Day	June 16
Summer Solstice	June 20
Independence Day	July 4
Labor Day	September 2
Autumnal Equinox	September 22
Daylight Saving Time Ends	November 3
Veterans Day	November 11
Thanksgiving Day	November 28
First Sunday of Advent	December 1
Winter Solstice	December 21
Christmas Eve	December 24
Christmas Day	December 25
Hanukkah Begins	December 25
New Year's Eve	December 31
Hanukkah Ends	January 2, 2025

2024

January

Therefore we do not lose heart, but though
our outer person is decaying, yet our inner person
is being renewed day by day. For our momentary,
light affliction is producing for us an eternal weight
of glory far beyond all comparison.

2 CORINTHIANS 4:16-17 NASB

My Goals for the Month

JANUARY AT A GLANCE

Sun	Mon	Tue	Wed	Thu	Fri	Sat
	1	2	3	4	5	6
7	8	9	10	11	12	13
14	15	16	17	18	19	20
21	22	23	24	25	26	27
28	29	30	31			

Motivation

A strong reason to accomplish something. Incentive to achieve.

What does MOTIVATION mean to you?

On a scale of 1 to 10, how motivated are you to complete tasks?

1 2 3 4 5 6 7 8 9 10

WHAT INCENTIVES ARE
YOUR BEST MOTIVATORS?

JANUARY

JANUARY 2024

S	M	T	W	T	F	S
	1	2	3	4	5	6
7	8	9	10	11	12	13
14	15	16	17	18	19	20
21	22	23	24	25	26	27
28	29	30	31			

FEBRUARY 2024

S	M	T	W	T	F	S
				1	2	3
4	5	6	7	8	9	10
11	12	13	14	15	16	17
18	19	20	21	22	23	24
25	26	27	28	29		

Prayer List	MONDAY 1	TUESDAY 2	WEDNESDAY 3

Priorities

I'm thankful for...

They who wait for the Lᴏʀᴅ shall
renew their strength; they shall
mount up with wings like eagles; they
shall run and not be weary;
they shall walk and not faint.

ISAIAH 40:31 ESV

THURSDAY 4	FRIDAY 5	SATURDAY 6	SUNDAY 7

JANUARY

JANUARY 2024

S	M	T	W	T	F	S
	1	2	3	4	5	6
7	8	9	10	11	12	13
14	15	16	17	18	19	20
21	22	23	24	25	26	27
28	29	30	31			

FEBRUARY 2024

S	M	T	W	T	F	S
				1	2	3
4	5	6	7	8	9	10
11	12	13	14	15	16	17
18	19	20	21	22	23	24
25	26	27	28	29		

Prayer List	MONDAY 8	TUESDAY 9	WEDNESDAY 10

Priorities

I'm thankful for...

Always give yourselves fully
to the work of the Lord,
because you know that your
labor in the Lord is not in vain.

1 CORINTHIANS 15:58 NIV

THURSDAY 11	FRIDAY 12	SATURDAY 13	SUNDAY 14

JANUARY

JANUARY 2024

S	M	T	W	T	F	S
	1	2	3	4	5	6
7	8	9	10	11	12	13
14	15	16	17	18	19	20
21	22	23	24	25	26	27
28	29	30	31			

FEBRUARY 2024

S	M	T	W	T	F	S
				1	2	3
4	5	6	7	8	9	10
11	12	13	14	15	16	17
18	19	20	21	22	23	24
25	26	27	28	29		

Prayer List	MONDAY **15**	TUESDAY **16**	WEDNESDAY **17**

Priorities

I'm thankful for...

The LORD is for me; he will help me.
It is better to take refuge in the LORD
than to trust in people.

PSALM 118:7-8 NLT

THURSDAY 18	FRIDAY 19	SATURDAY 20	SUNDAY 21

JANUARY

JANUARY 2024
S M T W T F S
1 2 3 4 5 6
7 8 9 10 11 12 13
14 15 16 17 18 19 20
21 22 23 24 25 26 27
28 29 30 31

FEBRUARY 2024
S M T W T F S
1 2 3
4 5 6 7 8 9 10
11 12 13 14 15 16 17
18 19 20 21 22 23 24
25 26 27 28 29

Prayer List	MONDAY **22**	TUESDAY **23**	WEDNESDAY **24**

Priorities

I'm thankful for...

I keep my eyes always on the LORD.
With him at my right hand,
I will not be shaken.

PSALM 16:8 NIV

THURSDAY 25	FRIDAY 26	SATURDAY 27	SUNDAY 28

JANUARY/
FEBRUARY

JANUARY 2024

S	M	T	W	T	F	S
	1	2	3	4	5	6
7	8	9	10	11	12	13
14	15	16	17	18	19	20
21	22	23	24	25	26	27
28	29	30	31			

FEBRUARY 2024

S	M	T	W	T	F	S
				1	2	3
4	5	6	7	8	9	10
11	12	13	14	15	16	17
18	19	20	21	22	23	24
25	26	27	28	29		

Prayer List

MONDAY	29	TUESDAY	30	WEDNESDAY	31

Priorities

I'm thankful for.....

....

....

....

....

....

Blessed is the one who finds wisdom,
and the one who gets understanding.

PROVERBS 3:13 ESV

THURSDAY 1	FRIDAY 2	SATURDAY 3	SUNDAY 4

To Do

- [ ]
- [ ]
- [ ]
- [ ]
- [ ]
- [ ]
- [ ]
- [ ]
- [ ]
- [ ]
- [ ]
- [ ]
- [ ]
- [ ]
- [ ]
- [ ]
- [ ]
- [ ]
- [ ]
- [ ]
- [ ]
- [ ]

Notes

SPACE TO CREATE

2024

February

With me are riches and honor,
enduring wealth and prosperity.
My fruit is better than fine gold;
what I yield surpasses choice silver.

PROVERBS 8:18-19 NIV

My Goals for the Month

FEBRUARY AT A GLANCE

Sun	Mon	Tue	Wed	Thu	Fri	Sat
				1	2	3
4	5	6	7	8	9	10
11	12	13	14	15	16	17
18	19	20	21	22	23	24
25	26	27	28	29		

Passion

Compelling emotion. Deep feeling. Strong enthusiasm.

What does PASSION mean to you?

On a scale of 1 to 10, how passionate are you about achieving your dreams?

WHAT HAVE YOU DONE LATELY
TO FUEL YOUR PASSION?

FEBRUARY

FEBRUARY 2024

S	M	T	W	T	F	S
				1	2	3
4	5	6	7	8	9	10
11	12	13	14	15	16	17
18	19	20	21	22	23	24
25	26	27	28	29		

MARCH 2024

S	M	T	W	T	F	S
					1	2
3	4	5	6	7	8	9
10	11	12	13	14	15	16
17	18	19	20	21	22	23
24	25	26	27	28	29	30
31						

Prayer List

MONDAY 5	TUESDAY 6	WEDNESDAY 7

Priorities

I'm thankful for...

THURSDAY 8	FRIDAY 9	SATURDAY 10	SUNDAY 11

FEBRUARY

FEBRUARY 2024

S	M	T	W	T	F	S
				1	2	3
4	5	6	7	8	9	10
11	12	13	14	15	16	17
18	19	20	21	22	23	24
25	26	27	28	29		

MARCH 2024

S	M	T	W	T	F	S
					1	2
3	4	5	6	7	8	9
10	11	12	13	14	15	16
17	18	19	20	21	22	23
24	25	26	27	28	29	30
31						

Prayer List

MONDAY **12**   TUESDAY **13**   WEDNESDAY **14**

Priorities

I'm thankful for...

THURSDAY 15	FRIDAY 16	SATURDAY 17	SUNDAY 18

FEBRUARY

FEBRUARY 2024

S	M	T	W	T	F	S
				1	2	3
4	5	6	7	8	9	10
11	12	13	14	15	16	17
18	19	20	21	22	23	24
25	26	27	28	29		

MARCH 2024

S	M	T	W	T	F	S
					1	2
3	4	5	6	7	8	9
10	11	12	13	14	15	16
17	18	19	20	21	22	23
24	25	26	27	28	29	30
31						

Prayer List	MONDAY **19**	TUESDAY **20**	WEDNESDAY **21**

Priorities

I'm thankful for...

THURSDAY 22	FRIDAY 23	SATURDAY 24	SUNDAY 25

FEBRUARY/ MARCH

FEBRUARY 2024

S	M	T	W	T	F	S
				1	2	3
4	5	6	7	8	9	10
11	12	13	14	15	16	17
18	19	20	21	22	23	24
25	26	27	28	29		

MARCH 2024

S	M	T	W	T	F	S
					1	2
3	4	5	6	7	8	9
10	11	12	13	14	15	16
17	18	19	20	21	22	23
24	25	26	27	28	29	30
31						

Prayer List	MONDAY 26	TUESDAY 27	WEDNESDAY 28

Priorities

I'm thankful for...

THURSDAY 29	FRIDAY 1	SATURDAY 2	SUNDAY 3

To Do

Notes

SPACE TO CREATE

2024

—

March

"You are the light of the world. A city set on a hill cannot be hidden. Nor do people light a lamp and put it under a basket, but on a stand, and it gives light to all in the house. In the same way, let your light shine before others, so that they may see your good works and give glory to your Father who is in heaven."

MATTHEW 5:14-16 ESV

My Goals for the Month

MARCH AT A GLANCE

Sun	Mon	Tue	Wed	Thu	Fri	Sat
					1	2
3	4	5	6	7	8	9
10	11	12	13	14	15	16
17	18	19	20	21	22	23
24 / 31	25	26	27	28	29	30

Integrity

Doing the right thing when no one is watching. Maintaining moral and ethical characteristics.

What does INTEGRITY mean to you?

On a scale of 1 to 10, how high does integrity rank on your character goals?

HOW DO YOU PRACTICE INTEGRITY IN DIFFICULT SITUATIONS?

MARCH

MARCH 2024
S	M	T	W	T	F	S
					1	2
3	4	5	6	7	8	9
10	11	12	13	14	15	16
17	18	19	20	21	22	23
24	25	26	27	28	29	30
31						

APRIL 2024
S	M	T	W	T	F	S
	1	2	3	4	5	6
7	8	9	10	11	12	13
14	15	16	17	18	19	20
21	22	23	24	25	26	27
28	29	30				

Prayer List	MONDAY 4	TUESDAY 5	WEDNESDAY 6

Priorities

I'm thankful for...

Let the sea and everything in it
shout his praise!
Let the earth and all
living things join in.

PSALM 98:7 NLT

THURSDAY 7	FRIDAY 8	SATURDAY 9	SUNDAY 10

MARCH

MARCH 2024

S	M	T	W	T	F	S
					1	2
3	4	5	6	7	8	9
10	11	12	13	14	15	16
17	18	19	20	21	22	23
24	25	26	27	28	29	30
31						

APRIL 2024

S	M	T	W	T	F	S
	1	2	3	4	5	6
7	8	9	10	11	12	13
14	15	16	17	18	19	20
21	22	23	24	25	26	27
28	29	30				

Prayer List	MONDAY **11**	TUESDAY **12**	WEDNESDAY **13**

Priorities

I'm thankful for...

I lie awake each night thinking of you
and reflecting on how you help me like
a father. I sing through the night under
your splendor-shadow, offering up to
you my songs of delight and joy!

PSALM 63:6-7 TPT

THURSDAY 14	FRIDAY 15	SATURDAY 16	SUNDAY 17

MARCH

MARCH 2024

S	M	T	W	T	F	S
					1	2
3	4	5	6	7	8	9
10	11	12	13	14	15	16
17	18	19	20	21	22	23
24	25	26	27	28	29	30
31						

APRIL 2024

S	M	T	W	T	F	S
	1	2	3	4	5	6
7	8	9	10	11	12	13
14	15	16	17	18	19	20
21	22	23	24	25	26	27
28	29	30				

Prayer List	MONDAY 18	TUESDAY 19	WEDNESDAY 20

Priorities

I'm thankful for...

THURSDAY 21	FRIDAY 22	SATURDAY 23	SUNDAY 24

MARCH

MARCH 2024

S	M	T	W	T	F	S
					1	2
3	4	5	6	7	8	9
10	11	12	13	14	15	16
17	18	19	20	21	22	23
24	25	26	27	28	29	30
31						

APRIL 2024

S	M	T	W	T	F	S
	1	2	3	4	5	6
7	8	9	10	11	12	13
14	15	16	17	18	19	20
21	22	23	24	25	26	27
28	29	30				

Prayer List	MONDAY 25	TUESDAY 26	WEDNESDAY 27

Priorities

I'm thankful for...

My child, don't lose sight of
common sense and discernment.
Hang on to them, for they
will refresh your soul.

PROVERBS 3:21-22 NLT

THURSDAY 28	FRIDAY 29	SATURDAY 30	SUNDAY 31

To Do

- [ ] ....
- [ ] ....
- [ ] ....
- [ ] ....
- [ ] ....
- [ ] ....
- [ ] ....
- [ ] ....
- [ ] ....
- [ ] ....
- [ ] ....
- [ ] ....
- [ ] ....
- [ ] ....
- [ ] ....
- [ ] ....
- [ ] ....
- [ ] ....
- [ ] ....
- [ ] ....
- [ ] ....

Notes

SPACE TO CREATE

2024
—
April

One thing I have desired of the LORD,

That will I seek:

That I may dwell in the house of the LORD

All the days of my life,

To behold the beauty of the LORD,

And to inquire in His temple.

PSALM 27:4 NKJV

My Goals for the Month

APRIL AT A GLANCE

Sun	Mon	Tue	Wed	Thu	Fri	Sat
	1	2	3	4	5	6
7	8	9	10	11	12	13
14	15	16	17	18	19	20
21	22	23	24	25	26	27
28	29	30				

Simplicity

Minimalistic. Not complex, busy, or chaotic. Easy.

What does SIMPLICITY mean to you?

On a scale of 1 to 10, how simply do you live?

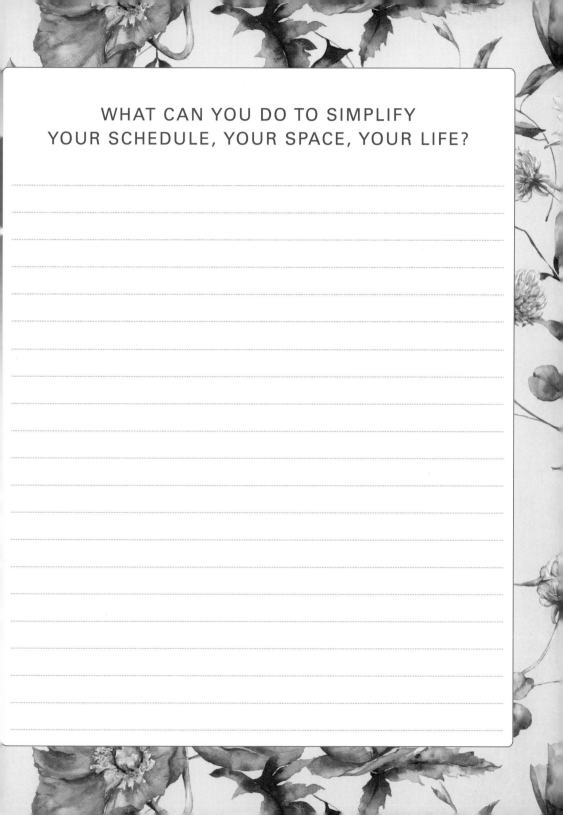

WHAT CAN YOU DO TO SIMPLIFY
YOUR SCHEDULE, YOUR SPACE, YOUR LIFE?

APRIL

APRIL 2024

S	M	T	W	T	F	S
	1	2	3	4	5	6
7	8	9	10	11	12	13
14	15	16	17	18	19	20
21	22	23	24	25	26	27
28	29	30				

MAY 2024

S	M	T	W	T	F	S
			1	2	3	4
5	6	7	8	9	10	11
12	13	14	15	16	17	18
19	20	21	22	23	24	25
26	27	28	29	30	31	

Prayer List	MONDAY 1	TUESDAY 2	WEDNESDAY 3

Priorities

I'm thankful for... ....

....

....

....

....

....

The steadfast love
of the LORD never ceases;
his mercies never come to an end.

LAMENTATIONS 3:22 ESV

THURSDAY 4	FRIDAY 5	SATURDAY 6	SUNDAY 7

APRIL

APRIL 2024

S	M	T	W	T	F	S
	1	2	3	4	5	6
7	8	9	10	11	12	13
14	15	16	17	18	19	20
21	22	23	24	25	26	27
28	29	30				

MAY 2024

S	M	T	W	T	F	S
			1	2	3	4
5	6	7	8	9	10	11
12	13	14	15	16	17	18
19	20	21	22	23	24	25
26	27	28	29	30	31	

Prayer List

MONDAY 8

TUESDAY 9

WEDNESDAY 10

Priorities

I'm thankful for...

THURSDAY 11	FRIDAY 12	SATURDAY 13	SUNDAY 14

APRIL

APRIL 2024
S	M	T	W	T	F	S
	1	2	3	4	5	6
7	8	9	10	11	12	13
14	15	16	17	18	19	20
21	22	23	24	25	26	27
28	29	30				

MAY 2024
S	M	T	W	T	F	S
			1	2	3	4
5	6	7	8	9	10	11
12	13	14	15	16	17	18
19	20	21	22	23	24	25
26	27	28	29	30	31	

Prayer List	MONDAY **15**	TUESDAY **16**	WEDNESDAY **17**

Priorities

I'm thankful for...

All the ways of the Lord are loving
and faithful for those who follow
the ways of his covenant.

PSALM 25:10 TPT

THURSDAY 18	FRIDAY 19	SATURDAY 20	SUNDAY 21

APRIL

APRIL 2024

S	M	T	W	T	F	S
	1	2	3	4	5	6
7	8	9	10	11	12	13
14	15	16	17	18	19	20
21	22	23	24	25	26	27
28	29	30				

MAY 2024

S	M	T	W	T	F	S
			1	2	3	4
5	6	7	8	9	10	11
12	13	14	15	16	17	18
19	20	21	22	23	24	25
26	27	28	29	30	31	

Prayer List

MONDAY 22 | **TUESDAY 23** | **WEDNESDAY 24**

Priorities

I'm thankful for...

This is the day the LORD has made;
We will rejoice and be glad in it.

PSALM 118:24 NKJV

THURSDAY 25	FRIDAY 26	SATURDAY 27	SUNDAY 28

To Do

- [ ]
- [ ]
- [ ]
- [ ]
- [ ]
- [ ]
- [ ]
- [ ]
- [ ]
- [ ]
- [ ]
- [ ]
- [ ]
- [ ]
- [ ]
- [ ]
- [ ]
- [ ]
- [ ]
- [ ]
- [ ]

Notes

SPACE TO CREATE

2024

—

May

Be truly glad! There is wonderful joy ahead....
You love him even though you have never seen him.
Though you do not see him now, you trust him;
and you rejoice with a glorious, inexpressible joy.

1 PETER 1:6, 8 NLT

My Goals for the Month

....

....

....

....

....

MAY AT A GLANCE

Sun	Mon	Tue	Wed	Thu	Fri	Sat
			1	2	3	4
5	6	7	8	9	10	11
12	13	14	15	16	17	18
19	20	21	22	23	24	25
26	27	28	29	30	31	

Balance

Equal distribution. Of symmetrical proportions. Equivalence of parts.

What does BALANCE mean to you?

On a scale of 1 to 10, how balanced is your life?

1 2 3 4 5 6 7 8 9 10

HOW CAN YOU REARRANGE THE PARTS OF YOUR LIFE TO CREATE BETTER BALANCE?

APRIL/ MAY

APRIL 2024
S	M	T	W	T	F	S
	1	2	3	4	5	6
7	8	9	10	11	12	13
14	15	16	17	18	19	20
21	22	23	24	25	26	27
28	29	30				

MAY 2024
S	M	T	W	T	F	S
			1	2	3	4
5	6	7	8	9	10	11
12	13	14	15	16	17	18
19	20	21	22	23	24	25
26	27	28	29	30	31	

Prayer List	MONDAY 29	TUESDAY 30	WEDNESDAY 1
Priorities			

I'm thankful for...

....

....

....

....

I remember what happened long ago;
I consider everything you have done.
I think about all you have made.

PSALM 143:5 NCV

THURSDAY 2	FRIDAY 3	SATURDAY 4	SUNDAY 5

MAY

MAY 2024

S	M	T	W	T	F	S
			1	2	3	4
5	6	7	8	9	10	11
12	13	14	15	16	17	18
19	20	21	22	23	24	25
26	27	28	29	30	31	

JUNE 2024

S	M	T	W	T	F	S
						1
2	3	4	5	6	7	8
9	10	11	12	13	14	15
16	17	18	19	20	21	22
23	24	25	26	27	28	29
30						

Prayer List	MONDAY 6	TUESDAY 7	WEDNESDAY 8
Priorities			

I'm thankful for...

THURSDAY 9	FRIDAY 10	SATURDAY 11	SUNDAY 12

MAY

MAY 2024

S	M	T	W	T	F	S
			1	2	3	4
5	6	7	8	9	10	11
12	13	14	15	16	17	18
19	20	21	22	23	24	25
26	27	28	29	30	31	

JUNE 2024

S	M	T	W	T	F	S
						1
2	3	4	5	6	7	8
9	10	11	12	13	14	15
16	17	18	19	20	21	22
23	24	25	26	27	28	29
30						

Prayer List

MONDAY 13	TUESDAY 14	WEDNESDAY 15

Priorities

I'm thankful for...

THURSDAY 16	FRIDAY 17	SATURDAY 18	SUNDAY 19

MAY

MAY 2024

S	M	T	W	T	F	S
			1	2	3	4
5	6	7	8	9	10	11
12	13	14	15	16	17	18
19	20	21	22	23	24	25
26	27	28	29	30	31	

JUNE 2024

S	M	T	W	T	F	S
						1
2	3	4	5	6	7	8
9	10	11	12	13	14	15
16	17	18	19	20	21	22
23	24	25	26	27	28	29
30						

Prayer List

MONDAY 20	TUESDAY 21	WEDNESDAY 22

Priorities

I'm thankful for...

THURSDAY 23	FRIDAY 24	SATURDAY 25	SUNDAY 26

MAY/ JUNE

MAY 2024

S	M	T	W	T	F	S
			1	2	3	4
5	6	7	8	9	10	11
12	13	14	15	16	17	18
19	20	21	22	23	24	25
26	27	28	29	30	31	

JUNE 2024

S	M	T	W	T	F	S
						1
2	3	4	5	6	7	8
9	10	11	12	13	14	15
16	17	18	19	20	21	22
23	24	25	26	27	28	29
30						

Prayer List	MONDAY 27	TUESDAY 28	WEDNESDAY 29

Priorities

I'm thankful for...

"Do not fear, for I am with you;
Do not be afraid, for I am your God.
I will strengthen you, I will also help
you, I will also uphold you with My
righteous right hand."

ISAIAH 41:10 NASB

THURSDAY 30	FRIDAY 31	SATURDAY 1	SUNDAY 2

To Do

Notes

SPACE TO CREATE

2024

June

Praise the LORD!
Praise God in his sanctuary;
praise him in his mighty heavens!
Praise him for his mighty deeds;
praise him according to his excellent greatness!
Let everything that has breath praise the LORD!
Praise the LORD!

PSALM 150:1-2, 6 ESV

My Goals for the Month

....

....

....

....

....

JUNE AT A GLANCE

Sun	Mon	Tue	Wed	Thu	Fri	Sat
						1
2	3	4	5	6	7	8
9	10	11	12	13	14	15
16	17	18	19	20	21	22
23 / 30	24	25	26	27	28	29

Empathy

Ability to identify with the feelings of others. Seeking to understand.

What does EMPATHY mean to you?

On a scale of 1 to 10, how empathetic are you toward others?

1 2 3 4 5 6 7 8 9 10

HOW DO YOU SHOW OTHERS YOUR CARE AND CONCERN FOR WHAT THEY ARE GOING THROUGH?

JUNE

JUNE 2024
S	M	T	W	T	F	S
						1
2	3	4	5	6	7	8
9	10	11	12	13	14	15
16	17	18	19	20	21	22
23	24	25	26	27	28	29
30						

JULY 2024
S	M	T	W	T	F	S
	1	2	3	4	5	6
7	8	9	10	11	12	13
14	15	16	17	18	19	20
21	22	23	24	25	26	27
28	29	30	31			

Prayer List	MONDAY 3	TUESDAY 4	WEDNESDAY 5

Priorities

I'm thankful for...

Those who live in the shelter
of the Most High
will find rest in the shadow
of the Almighty.

PSALM 91:1 NLT

THURSDAY 6	FRIDAY 7	SATURDAY 8	SUNDAY 9

JUNE

JUNE 2024

S	M	T	W	T	F	S
						1
2	3	4	5	6	7	8
9	10	11	12	13	14	15
16	17	18	19	20	21	22
23	24	25	26	27	28	29
30						

JULY 2024

S	M	T	W	T	F	S
	1	2	3	4	5	6
7	8	9	10	11	12	13
14	15	16	17	18	19	20
21	22	23	24	25	26	27
28	29	30	31			

Prayer List

MONDAY **10** | TUESDAY **11** | WEDNESDAY **12**

Priorities

I'm thankful for... ....

....

....

....

....

The LORD will keep you
from all harm—
he will watch over your life.

PSALM 121:7 NIV

THURSDAY 13	FRIDAY 14	SATURDAY 15	SUNDAY 16

JUNE

JUNE 2024

S	M	T	W	T	F	S
						1
2	3	4	5	6	7	8
9	10	11	12	13	14	15
16	17	18	19	20	21	22
23	24	25	26	27	28	29
30						

JULY 2024

S	M	T	W	T	F	S
	1	2	3	4	5	6
7	8	9	10	11	12	13
14	15	16	17	18	19	20
21	22	23	24	25	26	27
28	29	30	31			

Prayer List

MONDAY **17**

TUESDAY **18**

WEDNESDAY **19**

Priorities

I'm thankful for...

The heavens are yours;
the earth also is yours;
the world and all that is in it,
you have founded them.

PSALM 89:11 ESV

THURSDAY 20	FRIDAY 21	SATURDAY 22	SUNDAY 23

JUNE

JUNE 2024

S	M	T	W	T	F	S
						1
2	3	4	5	6	7	8
9	10	11	12	13	14	15
16	17	18	19	20	21	22
23	24	25	26	27	28	29
30						

JULY 2024

S	M	T	W	T	F	S
	1	2	3	4	5	6
7	8	9	10	11	12	13
14	15	16	17	18	19	20
21	22	23	24	25	26	27
28	29	30	31			

Prayer List	MONDAY 24	TUESDAY 25	WEDNESDAY 26
Priorities			

I'm thankful for......

....

....

....

....

....

"You are worthy, our Lord and God,
to receive glory and honor and power,
for you created all things,
and by your will they were created
and have their being."

REVELATION 4:11 NIV

THURSDAY 27	FRIDAY 28	SATURDAY 29	SUNDAY 30

To Do

Notes

SPACE TO CREATE

2024

—

July

O Lᴏʀᴅ, You have searched me and known me.

You know my sitting down and my rising up;

You understand my thought afar off.

You comprehend my path and my lying down,

And are acquainted with all my ways.

For there is not a word on my tongue,

But behold, O Lᴏʀᴅ, You know it altogether.

PSALM 139:1-4 NKJV

My Goals for the Month

....

....

....

....

....

JULY AT A GLANCE

Sun	Mon	Tue	Wed	Thu	Fri	Sat
	1	2	3	4	5	6
7	8	9	10	11	12	13
14	15	16	17	18	19	20
21	22	23	24	25	26	27
28	29	30	31			

Faith

Strong belief. Confidence.
Trust in God.

What does FAITH mean to you?

On a scale of 1 to 10, how important is faith to you?

1 2 3 4 5 6 7 8 9 10

WHAT CAN YOU DO TO ENCOURAGE YOUR FAITH JOURNEY THIS MONTH?

JULY

JULY 2024

S	M	T	W	T	F	S
	1	2	3	4	5	6
7	8	9	10	11	12	13
14	15	16	17	18	19	20
21	22	23	24	25	26	27
28	29	30	31			

AUGUST 2024

S	M	T	W	T	F	S
				1	2	3
4	5	6	7	8	9	10
11	12	13	14	15	16	17
18	19	20	21	22	23	24
25	26	27	28	29	30	31

Prayer List	MONDAY 1	TUESDAY 2	WEDNESDAY 3

Priorities

I'm thankful for...

Praise him, sun and moon;
praise him, all you shining stars.
Praise him, you highest heavens
and you waters above the skies.

PSALM 148:3-5 NIV

THURSDAY 4	FRIDAY 5	SATURDAY 6	SUNDAY 7

JULY

JULY 2024

S	M	T	W	T	F	S
	1	2	3	4	5	6
7	8	9	10	11	12	13
14	15	16	17	18	19	20
21	22	23	24	25	26	27
28	29	30	31			

AUGUST 2024

S	M	T	W	T	F	S
				1	2	3
4	5	6	7	8	9	10
11	12	13	14	15	16	17
18	19	20	21	22	23	24
25	26	27	28	29	30	31

Prayer List	MONDAY 8	TUESDAY 9	WEDNESDAY 10

Priorities

I'm thankful for...

THURSDAY 11	FRIDAY 12	SATURDAY 13	SUNDAY 14

JULY

JULY 2024

S	M	T	W	T	F	S
	1	2	3	4	5	6
7	8	9	10	11	12	13
14	15	16	17	18	19	20
21	22	23	24	25	26	27
28	29	30	31			

AUGUST 2024

S	M	T	W	T	F	S
				1	2	3
4	5	6	7	8	9	10
11	12	13	14	15	16	17
18	19	20	21	22	23	24
25	26	27	28	29	30	31

Prayer List

MONDAY **15** TUESDAY **16** WEDNESDAY **17**

Priorities

I'm thankful for...

....

....

....

....

He loves righteousness and justice;
The earth is full of the goodness
of the Lord.

PSALM 33:5 NKJV

THURSDAY 18	FRIDAY 19	SATURDAY 20	SUNDAY 21

JULY

JULY 2024

S	M	T	W	T	F	S
	1	2	3	4	5	6
7	8	9	10	11	12	13
14	15	16	17	18	19	20
21	22	23	24	25	26	27
28	29	30	31			

AUGUST 2024

S	M	T	W	T	F	S
				1	2	3
4	5	6	7	8	9	10
11	12	13	14	15	16	17
18	19	20	21	22	23	24
25	26	27	28	29	30	31

Prayer List	MONDAY **22**	TUESDAY **23**	WEDNESDAY **24**

Priorities

I'm thankful for...

THURSDAY 25	FRIDAY 26	SATURDAY 27	SUNDAY 28

JULY/ AUGUST

JULY 2024

S	M	T	W	T	F	S
	1	2	3	4	5	6
7	8	9	10	11	12	13
14	15	16	17	18	19	20
21	22	23	24	25	26	27
28	29	30	31			

AUGUST 2024

S	M	T	W	T	F	S
				1	2	3
4	5	6	7	8	9	10
11	12	13	14	15	16	17
18	19	20	21	22	23	24
25	26	27	28	29	30	31

Prayer List	MONDAY 29	TUESDAY 30	WEDNESDAY 31

Priorities

I'm thankful for...

....

....

....

....

The LORD directs the steps
of the godly.
He delights in every detail
of their lives.

PSALM 37:23 NLT

THURSDAY 1	FRIDAY 2	SATURDAY 3	SUNDAY 4

To Do

Notes

SPACE TO CREATE

2024

August

You keep him in perfect peace
whose mind is stayed on you,
because he trusts in you.

ISAIAH 26:3 ESV

My Goals for the Month

AUGUST AT A GLANCE

Sun	Mon	Tue	Wed	Thu	Fri	Sat
				1	2	3
4	5	6	7	8	9	10
11	12	13	14	15	16	17
18	19	20	21	22	23	24
25	26	27	28	29	30	31

Discipline

Self-controlled, purposeful actions. Strict routine for achieving a goal.

What does DISCIPLINE mean to you?

On a scale of 1 to 10, how disciplined are you?

1 2 3 4 5 6 7 8 9 10

HOW CAN YOU IMPLEMENT DISCIPLINE IN YOUR LIFE TO COMPLETE WHAT YOU SET OUT TO DO?

AUGUST

AUGUST 2024

S	M	T	W	T	F	S
				1	2	3
4	5	6	7	8	9	10
11	12	13	14	15	16	17
18	19	20	21	22	23	24
25	26	27	28	29	30	31

SEPTEMBER 2024

S	M	T	W	T	F	S
1	2	3	4	5	6	7
8	9	10	11	12	13	14
15	16	17	18	19	20	21
22	23	24	25	26	27	28
29	30					

Prayer List	MONDAY	5	TUESDAY	6	WEDNESDAY	7

Priorities

I'm thankful for...

Trust in the LORD with all your heart;
do not depend on
your own understanding.

PROVERBS 3:5 NLT

THURSDAY 8	FRIDAY 9	SATURDAY 10	SUNDAY 11

AUGUST

AUGUST 2024

S	M	T	W	T	F	S
				1	2	3
4	5	6	7	8	9	10
11	12	13	14	15	16	17
18	19	20	21	22	23	24
25	26	27	28	29	30	31

SEPTEMBER 2024

S	M	T	W	T	F	S
1	2	3	4	5	6	7
8	9	10	11	12	13	14
15	16	17	18	19	20	21
22	23	24	25	26	27	28
29	30					

Prayer List

MONDAY **12** TUESDAY **13** WEDNESDAY **14**

Priorities

I'm thankful for... ....
....
....
....
....
....

"Yours, O Lᴏʀᴅ, is the greatness
and the power and the glory
and the victory and the majesty,
for all that is in the heavens
and in the earth is yours."

1 CHRONICLES 29:11 ESV

THURSDAY 15	FRIDAY 16	SATURDAY 17	SUNDAY 18

AUGUST

AUGUST 2024

S	M	T	W	T	F	S
				1	2	3
4	5	6	7	8	9	10
11	12	13	14	15	16	17
18	19	20	21	22	23	24
25	26	27	28	29	30	31

SEPTEMBER 2024

S	M	T	W	T	F	S
1	2	3	4	5	6	7
8	9	10	11	12	13	14
15	16	17	18	19	20	21
22	23	24	25	26	27	28
29	30					

Prayer List	MONDAY **19**	TUESDAY **20**	WEDNESDAY **21**

Priorities

I'm thankful for...

The LORD is near to all
who call upon Him,
To all who call upon Him in truth.

PSALM 145:18 NKJV

THURSDAY 22	FRIDAY 23	SATURDAY 24	SUNDAY 25

AUGUST/ SEPTEMBER

AUGUST 2024

S	M	T	W	T	F	S
				1	2	3
4	5	6	7	8	9	10
11	12	13	14	15	16	17
18	19	20	21	22	23	24
25	26	27	28	29	30	31

SEPTEMBER 2024

S	M	T	W	T	F	S
1	2	3	4	5	6	7
8	9	10	11	12	13	14
15	16	17	18	19	20	21
22	23	24	25	26	27	28
29	30					

Prayer List	MONDAY 26	TUESDAY 27	WEDNESDAY 28

Priorities

I'm thankful for...

THURSDAY 29	FRIDAY 30	SATURDAY 31	SUNDAY 1

To Do

- ☐
- ☐
- ☐
- ☐
- ☐
- ☐
- ☐
- ☐
- ☐
- ☐
- ☐
- ☐
- ☐
- ☐
- ☐
- ☐
- ☐
- ☐
- ☐
- ☐

Notes

SPACE TO CREATE

2024

—

September

Surely you have granted him unending blessings
and made him glad with the joy of your presence.

PSALM 21:6 NIV

My Goals for the Month

....

....

....

....

....

SEPTEMBER AT A GLANCE

Sun	Mon	Tue	Wed	Thu	Fri	Sat
1	2	3	4	5	6	7
8	9	10	11	12	13	14
15	16	17	18	19	20	21
22	23	24	25	26	27	28
29	30					

Awareness

Being conscious of what is happening in and around you. Alert. Attentive. Perceptive. Observant.

What does AWARENESS mean to you?

On a scale of 1 to 10, how aware do you generally feel?

HOW COULD INCREASING YOUR AWARENESS LEAD TO BETTER RELATIONSHIPS WITH THE PEOPLE AROUND YOU?

SEPTEMBER

SEPTEMBER 2024

S	M	T	W	T	F	S
1	2	3	4	5	6	7
8	9	10	11	12	13	14
15	16	17	18	19	20	21
22	23	24	25	26	27	28
29	30					

OCTOBER 2024

S	M	T	W	T	F	S
		1	2	3	4	5
6	7	8	9	10	11	12
13	14	15	16	17	18	19
20	21	22	23	24	25	26
27	28	29	30	31		

Prayer List	MONDAY 2	TUESDAY 3	WEDNESDAY 4

Priorities

I'm thankful for...

Your word is like a lamp for my feet
and a light for my path.

PSALM 119:105 NCV

THURSDAY 5	FRIDAY 6	SATURDAY 7	SUNDAY 8

SEPTEMBER

SEPTEMBER 2024

S	M	T	W	T	F	S
1	2	3	4	5	6	7
8	9	10	11	12	13	14
15	16	17	18	19	20	21
22	23	24	25	26	27	28
29	30					

OCTOBER 2024

S	M	T	W	T	F	S
		1	2	3	4	5
6	7	8	9	10	11	12
13	14	15	16	17	18	19
20	21	22	23	24	25	26
27	28	29	30	31		

Prayer List	MONDAY 9	TUESDAY 10	WEDNESDAY 11

Priorities

I'm thankful for...

THURSDAY 12	FRIDAY 13	SATURDAY 14	SUNDAY 15

SEPTEMBER

SEPTEMBER 2024

S	M	T	W	T	F	S
1	2	3	4	5	6	7
8	9	10	11	12	13	14
15	16	17	18	19	20	21
22	23	24	25	26	27	28
29	30					

OCTOBER 2024

S	M	T	W	T	F	S
		1	2	3	4	5
6	7	8	9	10	11	12
13	14	15	16	17	18	19
20	21	22	23	24	25	26
27	28	29	30	31		

Prayer List	MONDAY 16	TUESDAY 17	WEDNESDAY 18

Priorities

I'm thankful for...

THURSDAY 19	FRIDAY 20	SATURDAY 21	SUNDAY 22

SEPTEMBER

SEPTEMBER 2024

S	M	T	W	T	F	S
1	2	3	4	5	6	7
8	9	10	11	12	13	14
15	16	17	18	19	20	21
22	23	24	25	26	27	28
29	30					

OCTOBER 2024

S	M	T	W	T	F	S
		1	2	3	4	5
6	7	8	9	10	11	12
13	14	15	16	17	18	19
20	21	22	23	24	25	26
27	28	29	30	31		

Prayer List

MONDAY 23	TUESDAY 24	WEDNESDAY 25

Priorities

I'm thankful for... ....

....

....

....

....

Send your light and your truth;

let them lead me.

Let them bring me

to your holy mountain,

to your dwelling place.

PSALM 43:3 CSB

THURSDAY 26	FRIDAY 27	SATURDAY 28	SUNDAY 29

To Do

- [ ] ....
- [ ] ....
- [ ] ....
- [ ] ....
- [ ] ....
- [ ] ....
- [ ] ....
- [ ] ....
- [ ] ....
- [ ] ....
- [ ] ....
- [ ] ....
- [ ] ....
- [ ] ....
- [ ] ....
- [ ] ....
- [ ] ....
- [ ] ....
- [ ] ....
- [ ] ....
- [ ] ....
- [ ] ....

Notes

SPACE TO CREATE

2024

—

October

The LORD will fulfill his purpose for me;
your steadfast love, O LORD, endures forever.
Do not forsake the work of your hands.

PSALM 138:8 ESV

My Goals for the Month

OCTOBER AT A GLANCE

Sun	Mon	Tue	Wed	Thu	Fri	Sat
		1	2	3	4	5
6	7	8	9	10	11	12
13	14	15	16	17	18	19
20	21	22	23	24	25	26
27	28	29	30	31		

Creativity

Ability to form or shape things. Unique talent that utilizes individual capabilities.

What does CREATIVITY mean to you?

On a scale of 1 to 10, how creative do you think you are?

1 2 3 4 5 6 7 8 9 10

WHAT THINGS COME EASILY TO YOU? HOW CAN YOU BETTER RECOGNIZE YOUR CREATIVE GIFTS?

SEPTEMBER/ OCTOBER

OCTOBER 2024

S	M	T	W	T	F	S
		1	2	3	4	5
6	7	8	9	10	11	12
13	14	15	16	17	18	19
20	21	22	23	24	25	26
27	28	29	30	31		

NOVEMBER 2024

S	M	T	W	T	F	S
					1	2
3	4	5	6	7	8	9
10	11	12	13	14	15	16
17	18	19	20	21	22	23
24	25	26	27	28	29	30

Prayer List

MONDAY 30

TUESDAY 1

WEDNESDAY 2

Priorities

I'm thankful for......
....
....
....
....

Can anything ever separate us from
Christ's love? No, despite all these
things, overwhelming victory is ours
through Christ, who loved us.

ROMANS 8:35, 37 NLT

THURSDAY 3	FRIDAY 4	SATURDAY 5	SUNDAY 6

OCTOBER

OCTOBER 2024

S	M	T	W	T	F	S
		1	2	3	4	5
6	7	8	9	10	11	12
13	14	15	16	17	18	19
20	21	22	23	24	25	26
27	28	29	30	31		

NOVEMBER 2024

S	M	T	W	T	F	S
					1	2
3	4	5	6	7	8	9
10	11	12	13	14	15	16
17	18	19	20	21	22	23
24	25	26	27	28	29	30

Prayer List

MONDAY 7	TUESDAY 8	WEDNESDAY 9

Priorities

I'm thankful for...

THURSDAY 10	FRIDAY 11	SATURDAY 12	SUNDAY 13

OCTOBER

OCTOBER 2024

S	M	T	W	T	F	S
		1	2	3	4	5
6	7	8	9	10	11	12
13	14	15	16	17	18	19
20	21	22	23	24	25	26
27	28	29	30	31		

NOVEMBER 2024

S	M	T	W	T	F	S
					1	2
3	4	5	6	7	8	9
10	11	12	13	14	15	16
17	18	19	20	21	22	23
24	25	26	27	28	29	30

Prayer List	MONDAY 14	TUESDAY 15	WEDNESDAY 16

Priorities

I'm thankful for...
....
....
....
....
....

He renews my strength.
He guides me along right paths,
bringing honor to his name.

PSALM 23:3 NLT

THURSDAY 17	FRIDAY 18	SATURDAY 19	SUNDAY 20

OCTOBER

OCTOBER 2024

S	M	T	W	T	F	S
		1	2	3	4	5
6	7	8	9	10	11	12
13	14	15	16	17	18	19
20	21	22	23	24	25	26
27	28	29	30	31		

NOVEMBER 2024

S	M	T	W	T	F	S
					1	2
3	4	5	6	7	8	9
10	11	12	13	14	15	16
17	18	19	20	21	22	23
24	25	26	27	28	29	30

Prayer List	MONDAY 21	TUESDAY 22	WEDNESDAY 23

Priorities

I'm thankful for...

Seek his will in all you do,
and he will show you
which path to take.

PROVERBS 3:6 NLT

THURSDAY 24	FRIDAY 25	SATURDAY 26	SUNDAY 27

OCTOBER/ NOVEMBER

OCTOBER 2024

S	M	T	W	T	F	S
		1	2	3	4	5
6	7	8	9	10	11	12
13	14	15	16	17	18	19
20	21	22	23	24	25	26
27	28	29	30	31		

NOVEMBER 2024

S	M	T	W	T	F	S
					1	2
3	4	5	6	7	8	9
10	11	12	13	14	15	16
17	18	19	20	21	22	23
24	25	26	27	28	29	30

Prayer List	MONDAY 28	TUESDAY 29	WEDNESDAY 30
Priorities			

I'm thankful for...

....

....

....

....

Thanks be to God

for his inexpressible gift!

2 CORINTHIANS 9:15 ESV

THURSDAY 31	FRIDAY 1	SATURDAY 2	SUNDAY 3

To Do

- [ ]
- [ ]
- [ ]
- [ ]
- [ ]
- [ ]
- [ ]
- [ ]
- [ ]
- [ ]
- [ ]
- [ ]
- [ ]
- [ ]
- [ ]
- [ ]
- [ ]
- [ ]
- [ ]
- [ ]

Notes

2024

—

November

Commit your work to the LORD,
and your plans will be established.

PROVERBS 16:3 ESV

My Goals for the Month

NOVEMBER AT A GLANCE

Sun	Mon	Tue	Wed	Thu	Fri	Sat
					1	2
3	4	5	6	7	8	9
10	11	12	13	14	15	16
17	18	19	20	21	22	23
24	25	26	27	28	29	30

Appreciation

Show gratitude. Acknowledge thankfulness. Express delight through recognition.

What does APPRECIATION mean to you?

On a scale of 1 to 10, how appreciative are you on any given day?

1 2 3 4 5 6 7 8 9 10

WHAT CAN YOU DO TO SHOW
YOUR APPRECIATION TO OTHERS?

NOVEMBER

NOVEMBER 2024

S	M	T	W	T	F	S
					1	2
3	4	5	6	7	8	9
10	11	12	13	14	15	16
17	18	19	20	21	22	23
24	25	26	27	28	29	30

DECEMBER 2024

S	M	T	W	T	F	S
1	2	3	4	5	6	7
8	9	10	11	12	13	14
15	16	17	18	19	20	21
22	23	24	25	26	27	28
29	30	31				

Prayer List	MONDAY 4	TUESDAY 5	WEDNESDAY 6

Priorities

I'm thankful for...

Every good and perfect gift is from above, coming down from the Father of the heavenly lights, who does not change like shifting shadows.

JAMES 1:17 NIV

THURSDAY 7	FRIDAY 8	SATURDAY 9	SUNDAY 10

NOVEMBER

NOVEMBER 2024

S	M	T	W	T	F	S
					1	2
3	4	5	6	7	8	9
10	11	12	13	14	15	16
17	18	19	20	21	22	23
24	25	26	27	28	29	30

DECEMBER 2024

S	M	T	W	T	F	S
1	2	3	4	5	6	7
8	9	10	11	12	13	14
15	16	17	18	19	20	21
22	23	24	25	26	27	28
29	30	31				

Prayer List	MONDAY 11	TUESDAY 12	WEDNESDAY 13

Priorities

I'm thankful for...

I am confident of this very thing,
that He who began a good work
among you will complete it by the
day of Christ Jesus.

PHILIPPIANS 1:6 NASB

THURSDAY 14	FRIDAY 15	SATURDAY 16	SUNDAY 17

NOVEMBER

NOVEMBER 2024
S	M	T	W	T	F	S
					1	2
3	4	5	6	7	8	9
10	11	12	13	14	15	16
17	18	19	20	21	22	23
24	25	26	27	28	29	30

DECEMBER 2024
S	M	T	W	T	F	S
1	2	3	4	5	6	7
8	9	10	11	12	13	14
15	16	17	18	19	20	21
22	23	24	25	26	27	28
29	30	31				

Prayer List

MONDAY **18**

TUESDAY **19**

WEDNESDAY **20**

Priorities

I'm thankful for......
....
....
....
....

Yet the LORD longs
to be gracious to you;
therefore he will rise up
to show you compassion.

ISAIAH 30:18 NIV

THURSDAY **21**	FRIDAY **22**	SATURDAY **23**	SUNDAY **24**

NOVEMBER/
DECEMBER

NOVEMBER 2024
S M T W T F S
                1 2
3 4 5 6 7 8 9
10 11 12 13 14 15 16
17 18 19 20 21 22 23
24 25 26 27 28 29 30

DECEMBER 2024
S M T W T F S
1 2 3 4 5 6 7
8 9 10 11 12 13 14
15 16 17 18 19 20 21
22 23 24 25 26 27 28
29 30 31

Prayer List	MONDAY 25	TUESDAY 26	WEDNESDAY 27

Priorities

I'm thankful for...

....

....

....

....

THURSDAY 28	FRIDAY 29	SATURDAY 30	SUNDAY 1

To Do

- [ ]
- [ ]
- [ ]
- [ ]
- [ ]
- [ ]
- [ ]
- [ ]
- [ ]
- [ ]
- [ ]
- [ ]
- [ ]
- [ ]
- [ ]
- [ ]
- [ ]
- [ ]
- [ ]
- [ ]
- [ ]

Notes

SPACE TO CREATE

2024

December

His divine power has granted to us
everything pertaining to life and godliness,
through the true knowledge of Him who
called us by His own glory and excellence.

2 PETER 1:3 NASB

My Goals for the Month

DECEMBER AT A GLANCE

Sun	Mon	Tue	Wed	Thu	Fri	Sat
1	2	3	4	5	6	7
8	9	10	11	12	13	14
15	16	17	18	19	20	21
22	23	24	25	26	27	28
29	30	31				

Generosity

Give abundantly. Share unselfishly. Lavish blessings.

What does GENEROSITY mean to you?

On a scale of 1 to 10, how generous are you?

1 2 3 4 5 6 7 8 9 10

WHAT CAN YOU DO TO SHOW GENEROSITY IN YOUR TIME, TALENTS, OR FINANCES AT THIS TIME OF THE YEAR?

DECEMBER

DECEMBER 2024
S	M	T	W	T	F	S
1	2	3	4	5	6	7
8	9	10	11	12	13	14
15	16	17	18	19	20	21
22	23	24	25	26	27	28
29	30	31				

JANUARY 2025
S	M	T	W	T	F	S
			1	2	3	4
5	6	7	8	9	10	11
12	13	14	15	16	17	18
19	20	21	22	23	24	25
26	27	28	29	30	31	

Prayer List	MONDAY	2	TUESDAY	3	WEDNESDAY	4

Priorities

I'm thankful for...

THURSDAY 5	FRIDAY 6	SATURDAY 7	SUNDAY 8

DECEMBER

DECEMBER 2024

S	M	T	W	T	F	S
1	2	3	4	5	6	7
8	9	10	11	12	13	14
15	16	17	18	19	20	21
22	23	24	25	26	27	28
29	30	31				

JANUARY 2025

S	M	T	W	T	F	S
			1	2	3	4
5	6	7	8	9	10	11
12	13	14	15	16	17	18
19	20	21	22	23	24	25
26	27	28	29	30	31	

Prayer List	MONDAY 9	TUESDAY 10	WEDNESDAY 11

Priorities

I'm thankful for...

THURSDAY 12	FRIDAY 13	SATURDAY 14	SUNDAY 15

DECEMBER

DECEMBER 2024

S	M	T	W	T	F	S
1	2	3	4	5	6	7
8	9	10	11	12	13	14
15	16	17	18	19	20	21
22	23	24	25	26	27	28
29	30	31				

JANUARY 2025

S	M	T	W	T	F	S
			1	2	3	4
5	6	7	8	9	10	11
12	13	14	15	16	17	18
19	20	21	22	23	24	25
26	27	28	29	30	31	

Prayer List

MONDAY **16**　TUESDAY **17**　WEDNESDAY **18**

Priorities

I'm thankful for...

Jesus Christ is the same yesterday
and today, and forever.

HEBREWS 13:8 NASB

THURSDAY 19	FRIDAY 20	SATURDAY 21	SUNDAY 22

DECEMBER

DECEMBER 2024

S	M	T	W	T	F	S
	1	2	3	4	5	6	7
8	9	10	11	12	13	14
15	16	17	18	19	20	21
22	23	24	25	26	27	28
29	30	31

JANUARY 2025

S	M	T	W	T	F	S
			1	2	3	4
5	6	7	8	9	10	11
12	13	14	15	16	17	18
19	20	21	22	23	24	25
26	27	28	29	30	31

Prayer List	MONDAY **23**	TUESDAY **24**	WEDNESDAY **25**
Priorities			

I'm thankful for...

THURSDAY 26	FRIDAY 27	SATURDAY 28	SUNDAY 29

DECEMBER/
JANUARY

DECEMBER 2024
S	M	T	W	T	F	S
1	2	3	4	5	6	7
8	9	10	11	12	13	14
15	16	17	18	19	20	21
22	23	24	25	26	27	28
29	30	31				

JANUARY 2025
S	M	T	W	T	F	S
				1	2	3	4
5	6	7	8	9	10	11
12	13	14	15	16	17	18
19	20	21	22	23	24	25
26	27	28	29	30	31	

Prayer List	MONDAY 30	TUESDAY 31	WEDNESDAY 1

Priorities

I'm thankful for.....
....
....
....
....
....

For God has not given us
a spirit of fear, but of power
and of love and of a sound mind.

2 TIMOTHY 1:7 NKJV

THURSDAY 2	FRIDAY 3	SATURDAY 4	SUNDAY 5

To Do

Notes

SPACE TO CREATE

Bible Promises

ABILITY

We are not saying that we can do this work ourselves. It is God who makes us able to do all that we do.
2 Corinthians 3:5 NCV

Take a new grip with your tired hands and strengthen your weak knees. Mark out a straight path for your feet so that those who are weak and lame will not fall but become strong.
Hebrews 12:12-13 NLT

"My grace is sufficient for you, for my power is made perfect in weakness." Therefore I will boast all the more gladly of my weaknesses, so that the power of Christ may rest upon me.
2 Corinthians 12:9 ESV

ACCEPTANCE

"The Father gives me the people who are mine. Every one of them will come to me, and I will always accept them."
John 6:37 NCV

And he chose us to be his very own, joining us to himself even before he laid the foundation of the universe! Because of his great love, he ordained us, so that we would be seen as holy in his eyes with an unstained innocence.
Ephesians 1:4 TPT

ANGER

A gentle answer deflects anger,
but harsh words make tempers flare.
Proverbs 15:1 NLT

In your hearts revere Christ as Lord. Always be prepared to give an answer to everyone who asks you to give the reason for the hope that you have. But do this with gentleness and respect.
1 Peter 3:15 NIV

"Blessed are the gentle, for they will inherit the earth."
Matthew 5:5 NASB

Let your gentleness be evident to all. The Lord is near.
Philippians 4:5 NIV

ANXIETY

"Don't let your heart be troubled. Believe in God; believe also in me."
John 14:1 CSB

Cast all your anxiety on him because he cares for you.
1 Peter 5:7 NIV

Be still, and know that I am God.
I will be exalted among the nations,
I will be exalted in the earth!
Psalm 46:10 ESV

Do not be anxious about anything, but in every situation, by prayer and petition, with thanksgiving, present your requests to God.
Philippians 4:6 NIV

ASSURANCE

Your promises have been thoroughly tested,
and your servant loves them.
My eyes stay open through the watches of the night,
that I may meditate on your promises.
Psalm 119:140, 148 NIV

He has granted to us his precious and very great promises, so that through them you may become partakers of the divine nature, having escaped from the corruption that is in the world.
2 Peter 1:3-4 ESV

To him who is able to do immeasurably more than all we ask or imagine, according to his power that is at work within us, to him be glory...for ever and ever! Amen.
Ephesians 3:20–21 NIV

COMFORT

I will give them a crown to replace their ashes,
and the oil of gladness to replace their sorrow,
and clothes of praise to replace their spirit of sadness.
Then they will be called Trees of Goodness,
trees planted by the LORD to show his greatness.
      Isaiah 61:3 NCV

May your unfailing love be my comfort,
according to your promise to your servant.
      Psalm 119:76 NIV

May our Lord Jesus Christ himself and God our Father, who loved us and by his grace gave
us eternal comfort and a wonderful hope, comfort you and strengthen you.
      2 Thessalonians 2:16–17 NLT

CONFIDENCE

Be my rock of refuge,
to which I can always go;
give the command to save me,
for you are my rock and my fortress.
You have been my hope, Sovereign LORD,
my confidence since my youth.
      Psalm 71:3, 5 NIV

This is the confidence that we have toward him, that if we ask anything according to his
will he hears us. And if we know that he hears us in whatever we ask, we know that we have
the requests that we have asked of him.
      1 John 5:14–15 ESV

Let us then approach God's throne of grace with confidence, so that we may receive mercy
and find grace to help us in our time of need.
      Hebrews 4:16 NIV

COURAGE

So be strong and courageous,
all you who put your hope in the LORD!
      Psalm 31:24 NLT

May he give you the power to accomplish all the good things your faith prompts you to do.
2 Thessalonians 1:11 NLT

*"Be strong and courageous. Do not be frightened, and do not be dismayed, for the L*ORD *your God is with you wherever you go."*
Joshua 1:9 ESV

DILIGENCE

The plans of the diligent lead to profit
as surely as haste leads to poverty.
Proverbs 21:5 NIV

In all the work you are doing, work the best you can. Work as if you were doing it for the Lord, not for people.
Colossians 3:23 NCV

Be diligent in these matters; give yourself wholly to them, so that everyone may see your progress.
1 Timothy 4:15 NIV

ENCOURAGEMENT

The humble will see their God at work and be glad.
Let all who seek God's help be encouraged.
Psalm 69:32 NLT

We do not lose heart, but though our outer person is decaying, yet our inner person is being renewed day by day. For our momentary, light affliction is producing for us an eternal weight of glory far beyond all comparison.
2 Corinthians 4:16–17 NASB

Let us consider how to stir up one another to love and good works, not neglecting to meet together, as is the habit of some, but encouraging one another.
Hebrews 10:24–25 ESV

FAITH

Faith is confidence in what we hope for and assurance about what we do not see.
Hebrews 11:1 NIV

"Now behold, today I am going the way of all the earth, and you know in all your hearts and in all your souls that not one word of all the good words which the Lord your God spoke concerning you has failed; they all have been fulfilled for you, not one of them has failed."
Joshua 23:14 NASB

Faith comes by hearing, and hearing by the word of God.
Romans 10:17 NKJV

"If you have faith like a grain of mustard seed, you will say to this mountain, 'Move from here to there,' and it will move, and nothing will be impossible for you."
Matthew 17:20 ESV

FEAR

Where God's love is, there is no fear, because God's love drives out fear.
1 John 4:18 NCV

"Don't be afraid, for I am with you.
Don't be discouraged, for I am your God.
I will strengthen you and help you.
I will hold you up with my victorious right hand."
Isaiah 41:10 NLT

The Lord is my light and my salvation;
whom shall I fear?
The Lord is the stronghold of my life;
of whom shall I be afraid?
Psalm 27:1 ESV

FORGIVENESS

For You, Lord, are good, and ready to forgive,
And abundant in mercy to all those who call upon You.
Psalm 86:5 NKJV

As far as the east is from the west,
So far has He removed our wrongdoings from us.
Psalm 103:12 NASB

If we confess our sins, He is faithful and just to forgive us our sins and to cleanse us from all unrighteousness.
1 John 1:9 NKJV

My sacrifice, O God, is a broken spirit;
a broken and contrite heart
you, God, will not despise.
      Psalm 51:17 NIV

FREEDOM

Now that you have been set free from sin and have become slaves of God, the benefit
you reap leads to holiness, and the result is eternal life.
      Romans 6:22 NIV

"If you hold to my teaching, you are really my disciples. Then you will know the truth,
and the truth will set you free."
      John 8:31–32 NIV

Christ has truly set us free. Now make sure that you stay free, and don't get tied up
again in slavery to the law.
      Galatians 5:1 NLT

GUIDANCE

The LORD directs the steps of the godly.
He delights in every detail of their lives.
Though they stumble, they will never fall,
for the LORD holds them by the hand.
      Psalm 37:23–24 NLT

We know that all things work together for good to those who love God, to those who
are the called according to His purpose.
      Romans 8:28 NKJV

We can make our plans,
but the LORD determines our steps.
      Proverbs 16:9 NLT

HEALING

He was pierced for our transgressions, he was crushed for our iniquities;
the punishment that brought us peace was on him, and by his wounds we are healed.
      Isaiah 53:5 NIV

He said to her, "Daughter, your faith has made you well;
go in peace and be cured of your disease."
　　　Mark 5:34 NASB

My child, pay attention to what I say.
Listen carefully to my words.
Don't lose sight of them.
Let them penetrate deep into your heart,
for they bring life to those who find them,
and healing to their whole body.
　　　Proverbs 4:20–22 NLT

HONESTY

Truthful words stand the test of time,
but lies are soon exposed.
　　　Proverbs 12:19 NLT

"When he, the Spirit of truth, comes, he will guide you into all the truth."
　　　John 16:13 NIV

You desire truth in the innermost being,
And in secret You will make wisdom known to me.
　　　Psalm 51:6 NASB

HOPE

The Lord is good to those whose hope is in him,
to the one who seeks him.
　　　Lamentations 3:25 NIV

Blessed be the God and Father of our Lord Jesus Christ! According to his great mercy, he has
caused us to be born again to a living hope through the resurrection of Jesus Christ.
　　　1 Peter 1:3 ESV

May the God of hope fill you with all joy and peace as you trust in him, so that you may
overflow with hope by the power of the Holy Spirit.
　　　Romans 15:13 NIV

HUMILITY

Humility is the fear of the LORD;
its wages are riches and honor and life.
    Proverbs 22:4 NIV

Those who accept correction gain understanding.
Respect for the LORD will teach you wisdom.
If you want to be honored, you must be humble.
    Proverbs 15:32–33 NCV

In your relationships with one another, have the same mindset as Christ Jesus: Who, being
in very nature God, did not consider equality with God something to be used to his own
advantage; rather, he made himself nothing by taking the very nature of a servant, being
made in human likeness.
    Philippians 2:5-7 NIV

LONELINESS

The LORD is near to all who call on him,
to all who call on him in truth.
    Psalm 145:18 NIV

"Here I am! I stand at the door and knock. If anyone hears my voice and opens
the door, I will come in and eat with that person, and they with me."
    Revelation 3:20 NIV

"Behold, I am with you always, to the end of the age."
    Matthew 28:20 ESV

JOY

The LORD has done great things for us,
and we are filled with joy.
    Psalm 126:3 NIV

Satisfy us in the morning with your unfailing love,
that we may sing for joy and be glad all our days.
    Psalm 90:14 NIV

Be truly glad. There is wonderful joy ahead.... You love him even though you have never seen him. Though you do not see him now, you trust him; and you rejoice with a glorious, inexpressible joy.
1 Peter 1:6, 8 NLT

"Ask and you will receive, and your joy will be complete."
John 16:24 NIV

PATIENCE

As a prisoner for the Lord, then, I urge you to live a life worthy of the calling you have received. Be completely humble and gentle; be patient, bearing with one another in love.
Ephesians 4:1-2 NIV

"They are those who, hearing the word, hold it fast in an honest and good heart, and bear fruit with patience."
Luke 8:15 ESV

Imitate those who through faith and patience inherit what has been promised.
Hebrews 6:12 NIV

PEACE

*"These things I have spoken to you so that in Me you may have peace.
In the world you have tribulation, but take courage; I have overcome the world."*
John 16:33 NASB

*The LORD will give strength to His people;
The LORD will bless His people with peace.*
Psalm 29:11 NKJV

*"Peace I leave with you; my peace I give you. I do not give to you as the world gives.
Do not let your hearts be troubled and do not be afraid."*
John 14:27 NIV

PERSEVERANCE

God blesses those who patiently endure testing and temptation. Afterward they will receive the crown of life that God has promised to those who love him.
James 1:12 NLT

Let us not grow weary of doing good, for in due season we will reap,
if we do not give up.
    Galatians 6:9 ESV

Consider it pure joy...whenever you face trials of many kinds, because you know that
the testing of your faith develops perseverance. Let perseverance finish its work so
that you may be mature and complete, not lacking anything.
    James 1:2–4 NIV

PROTECTION

The LORD himself goes before you and will be with you;
he will never leave you nor forsake you.
    Deuteronomy 31:8 NIV

If you make the LORD your refuge,
if you make the Most High your shelter,
no evil will conquer you;
no plague will come near your home.
For he will order his angels
to protect you wherever you go.
    Psalm 91:9–11 NLT

PROVISION

God is able to make every grace overflow to you, so that in every way, always having
everything you need, you may excel in every good work.
    2 Corinthians 9:8 CSB

The LORD is all I need.
He takes care of me.
My share in life has been pleasant;
my part has been beautiful.
    Psalm 16:5–6 NCV

Whoever pursues righteousness and love
finds life, prosperity and honor.
    Proverbs 21:21 NIV

REWARD

Do not lose the courage you had in the past, which has a great reward. You must hold on, so you can do what God wants and receive what he has promised.
    Hebrews 10:35–36 NCV

Watch yourselves, so that you may not lose what we have worked for, but may win a full reward.
    2 John 1:8 ESV

"Look, I am coming soon! My reward is with me, and I will give to each person according to what they have done."
    Revelation 22:12 NIV

STRENGTH

Whom have I in heaven but you?
And earth has nothing I desire besides you.
My flesh and my heart may fail,
but God is the strength of my heart
and my portion forever.
    Psalm 73:25–26 NIV

Live as citizens of heaven, conducting yourselves in a manner worthy of the Good News about Christ...standing together with one spirit and one purpose, fighting together for the faith. Don't be intimidated in any way by your enemies. This will be a sign to them that you are going to be saved, even by God himself.
    Philippians 1:27–28 NLT

THANKFULNESS

Thanks be to God for his indescribable gift!
    2 Corinthians 9:15 NIV

Always be thankful. Let the message about Christ, in all its richness, fill your lives.
    Colossians 3:15 NLT

In everything give thanks; for this is the will of God for you in Christ Jesus.
    1 Thessalonians 5:18 NASB

WISDOM

If any of you lacks wisdom, you should ask God, who gives generously to all without finding fault, and it will be given to you.
James 1:5 NIV

For this reason we also, since the day we heard about it, have not ceased praying for you and asking that you may be filled with the knowledge of His will in all spiritual wisdom and understanding, so that you will walk in a manner worthy of the Lord, to please Him in all respects, bearing fruit in every good work and increasing in the knowledge of God.
Colossians 1:9-10 NASB

The wisdom from above is first of all pure. It is also peace loving, gentle at all times, and willing to yield to others. It is full of mercy and good deeds. It shows no favoritism and is always sincere.
James 3:17 NLT

WORRY

"Which of you by worrying can add a day to his life's span?"
Luke 12:25 NASB

Don't worry about anything; instead, pray about everything. Tell God what you need, and thank him for all he has done. Then you will experience God's peace, which exceeds anything we can understand. His peace will guard your hearts and minds as you live in Christ Jesus.
Philippians 4:6–7 NLT

Give your burdens to the Lord,
and he will take care of you.
Psalm 55:22 NLT

SPACE TO CREATE

SPACE TO CREATE

SPACE TO CREATE

SPACE TO CREATE

SPACE TO CREATE

SPACE TO CREATE

SPACE TO CREATE